AF333304

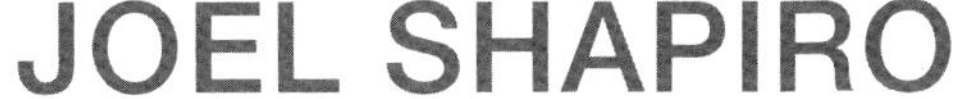

JOEL SHAPIRO

JOEL SHAPIRO

SCULPTURE AND DRAWINGS

MARCH 15 - APRIL 20, 1996

PACEWILDENSTEIN LOS ANGELES 9540 WILSHIRE BLVD. BEVERLY HILLS CA

JOEL SHAPIRO AND FIGURATIVE SCULPTURE

By Michael Brenson

Joel Shapiro is passionate about modernist figurative sculpture. He speaks with open admiration about Auguste Rodin, Henri Matisse and Pablo Picasso. He describes Alberto Giacometti as "the sculptor of the century."[1] In response to a question about Marcel Duchamp, he makes clear that it is with these figurative sculptors that he feels he belongs. "He's a brilliant artist," Shapiro says. "I mean, his work is phenomenal, but it's not a vein that I'm interested in. I have no choice. I'm involved in a more humanist pursuit, for better or worse. There's such history behind figurative sculpture. So many brilliant people have been doing it. Geniuses. Giacometti. Matisse. Picasso. It's not a question of whether you think they're good or not; they're beyond good. They're consummate, profound artists."

The connections between the figurative tradition in modernist sculpture and the sculptures Shapiro has been creating during the past 15 years are unmistakable. Shapiro's materials are wood, plaster and bronze, which were staples of modernist sculpture in the late 19th and early 20th centuries. His constructions and assemblages of rectangles carry within them the memory of the startling sculptural equilibrium of Matisse's *Large Seated Nude* and the gestural originality of his *Serpentine*. They suggest the playfulness and the openness to process essential to the creativity and content of Picasso's work, as well as the freedom with which Picasso erected a core volume and then affixed to or embedded objects into it. Shapiro's figures are equally hard to imagine without Giacometti's modesty and intimacy and ability to make standing, walking, sitting or running seem at once the most common, dignified and revealing of acts.

Like each of these modernists, and like another modernist sculptor he admires, Constantin Brancusi, who made the dialogue between abstraction and figuration so fertile that many sculptors continue to explore it, Shapiro believes deeply in form. He is fully attentive to surface, edge, shape and volume and makes the viewer's attentiveness to the language of sculpture essential to the experience his sculpture offers. He finds inexhaustible sources of insight and movement in the interrelationships of gravity and flight, expansion and contraction, stability and precariousness. He values each step of the working process, from the rough sculptural sketch in which a few small strips of wood are slapped together, to the refinement of proportions and shape and the enlargement of scale, to the life-size or larger works bolted into or sprawled across the floors of galleries, and now, increasingly, to the huge cast and welded Shapiros the non-art public can encounter on a busy street, in a corporate lobby, or outside a museum.

One of the most important distinctions between modernist figurative sculpture and other prominent modernist developments, like Constructivism and abstraction, is that the sculptures of Rodin, Matisse, Giacometti and Picasso are not utopian. Even if one or more of these artists were drawn to ideas of social progress and transformation, they did not put their sculpture in the service of them. They were very much concerned with the here and now — with the physical and psychological vibrations of people close to them, with spatial and psychological pressure, with the elegance and sensuality of a face or flower, with the feeling and structure of a head or back, with the ability of the human body to communicate responses and feelings so basic that almost anyone in the presence of their images could find in them echoes of their own situation.

Shapiro's sculptures are not instruments of a cause. They are conceived apart from any social, political or ideological uses to which human beings can be put. They acknowledge context but are not contextual. The rectangular boxes of which they are composed incorporate the surrounding architecture into the figures rather than demanding that the figures be understood in terms of their surroundings. Their emphasis is not on how the environment determines the individual but on how the individual shapes the environment. They reflect an aversion to hard-core ideology and group thinking that is characteristic of Shapiro's post-Minimalist generation, born during World War II and the Holocaust, when totalitarian destruction was fueled by obedience and generalization. Shapiro offers a vision of the human body as a physical and spiritual organism that changes so constantly and has so many sides that it can never be definitively categorized or controlled. Shifting identity is an essential part of their nature. So is movement. So is rootlessness. Shapiro's figures are architectural building blocks that could be adjusted to any occasion: they are their own homes. Camouflage and self-defense are part of their nature as well. They may pull viewers in through the intensity of their delight or pain but they can also hold them at bay through their projecting volumes and indifference to touch. Unlike Giacometti's figures, which are at times besieged by space, Shapiro offers a vision of the individual body as an organism with such powers of metamorphosis and self-reliance that it can clearly hold its own against politics and history. His figures are what they are and where they are completely, but they are also, always, something and somewhere else. It is their capacity for transformation not in the future, although this is an important part of their potential, but in the moment, and from moment to moment, that endows them with the capacity for survival and revelation.

So despite his unapologetic enthusiasm for Matisse, Picasso and Giacometti, Shapiro resists as much as he accepts the modernism he loves. With all his affection for Giacometti, his work is not concerned with ultimate questions, ultimate meanings. With all his respect for Brancusi, he does not make objects for prayerful contemplation. And while he may feel at ease with the word genius, which was part of the romance of modernist criticism and which makes post-modernists cringe, he has the post-modern aversion to the idea of a masterpiece. "The idea of a single piece that's *the* great piece is nonsense," he says. And he has the post-modern distrust of the heroic, although he frequently flirts with heroic associations, both in the size of his public commissions, and in his sculptural rhetoric, which can suggest an unconquerable stride or man triumphing over death.

In addition, while Shapiro uses early modernist materials, he uses them in decidedly non-modernist ways. There is no mystique of materials in his figurative work — no alluring tactility, no monolithic core that draws viewers in. Nor is there truth to materials. Plaster can be shaped by wood. Plaster can resemble wood. Three kinds of wood — fir, poplar and pine — were combined in one sculpture in this show, and it is hard to tell the difference between them. It can also be hard to tell the difference between his wood and bronze surfaces. Bronze is used not to develop indestructible commodities, although they may become that, but rather, most of the time, to insist upon form. In Shapiro's approach to materials, as in his approach to imagery, everything is at all times capable of emerging from and flowing into something else.

One of the clearest distinctions between the idea of the individual in Shapiro and the idea of the individual in Rodin and Giacometti lies in Shapiro's resistance to the idea of a single inviolable identity. His figures have multiple selves. Because they are usually a composite of several distinct and equally forceful psychological responses and physical states, they may acknowledge, but they always resist, the notions of tragedy and fate that run through Rodin and Giacometti and so much other European art. Even when it is clear that something irrevocable has been done to them, Shapiro's figures change course, enter another state, and by so doing, leave destiny, which may have thought it had them in its grip, behind.

In short, with all its respect for tradition and the individual, Shapiro's work is consistently surprising. It is also complex in ways that have barely begun to be investigated. And there is a radical dimension to it, one shaped by Jewish memory of the Holocaust and a particularly American notion of democracy and freedom. I want this essay to locate where that radicality is.

II

What is a Shapiro figure? How does it work? How are its meanings communicated by its sculptural language?

The vocabulary is basic. Shapiro works with rectangular boxes, usually substantially elongated. They are entirely assembled, that is to say, the four rectangular and two square sides are cut and worked separately and then joined.

The flat pieces of wood are so plain that they could not seem more ordinary, more matter-of-fact, but when they assume their place in boxes joined to other boxes they become evocative. They can suggest the limbs, torso and head of a body. They can suggest both architectural and children's building blocks. They can bring to mind, as well, the trunks and limbs of trees. Because of their hint of boys' toys and their absence of softness and curves, the figures usually seem male, but most of their gestures and emotions belong to women as well as men, and there is occasionally a sense of a man and woman locked together in the same configuration.

The rectangular boxes are essential to one of the key aspects of the work, the fluid relationship between figuration and abstraction. They enable Shapiro to build sculptures that are clearly figurative, and they enable him to build sculptures, like several of those in this show, that seem figurative but whose exact shapes and movements are hard to define. The rectangles make clear that the sculptures never pretend to be what they suggest or represent. Their geometry acknowledges the Minimalism that was the main force in sculpture as Shapiro was coming of age even as joining rectangular boxes into figurative constructions asserts his wish to make sculpture that is more supple and referential. The constructions of rectangles also encourage viewers to consider the process by which each sculpture was made, including the formal decisions so important to its energy and content.

If the vocabulary is elementary yet loaded with feeling and information, so is the movement the rectangles suggest. Walking, running, dancing, falling, tripping, tumbling are some of the basic actions Shapiro explores. Invariably, however, there is more than one action in the same construction, sometimes within the same point of view. A figure is on its feet, firmly on the ground, but it may also be standing on its head, its feet spread in the air. The same figure may pull back or hurl itself forward. Sometimes the same movement or gesture evokes different, even conflicting, responses. A figure's legs are splayed and one arm raised like a singer at a triumphant moment, but the arm also suggests a call for help by a dying man. In Shapiro's world, up can become down, front back, legs arms, foot head. Victory can become inseparable from defeat, entrapment from release, exuberance from melancholy. Elementary movements and basic shapes become human and poetic mysteries.

This multi-sidedness and interconnectedness would not be so compelling without Shapiro's ability to immerse his figures in each emotion or action. Whatever their responses or movements, they are engaged in them so totally that nothing else matters; nothing else even exists. Shapiro has a special understanding of the mechanics of the body and, in particular, of its spasmodic intensity when consumed by a particular emotion or event. Whatever activities or feelings his figures express, they have lurched or launched into them with such finality that their entire bodies are expressions of them. In a Shapiro sculpture each emotion or action seems so absolute that it is a condition, even as it flips into another emotion or action and reveals itself to be just one of the complex of states that constitutes a human being.

The conviction of these figures also depends upon Shapiro's incorporation of many experiences of time. For example, a vertical or diagonal rectangle may seem to have been positioned with great deliberation. But a diagonal attached to it may have emerged and been joined a little more quickly. And a diagonal rectangle attached to that may have taken its place even faster. Finally, a rectangle at shoulder or neck height may have been rammed into the construction so that its presence adds a note of impulsiveness, even rashness. Very rarely do all the rectangles in a Shapiro construction suggest the same timing. This distinctiveness within the sculptural process strengthens the identity of each part as it becomes part of the whole.

Just as important is Shapiro's ability to build into his figures an awareness of different ages. His surfaces may be pristine, cut slowly or quickly, or marked by the whorls of a circular saw that can make the wood seem etched by history. The smooth or worn surfaces suggest, along with the associations of the building blocks with architecture and with games, both a child's and an adult's experience. So do movements, which can range from a child's carefree running, to an adolescent's self-conscious performing, to an adult's methodical laboring. So does the way the sculptures point both toward the ground and up into space and therefore reach out to different sizes of people. So does the sense of a child's hypnotic absorption communicated by a body that is adolescent or adult in size.

How to combine finality with fluidity has been one of the prevailing issues of 20th-century sculpture. Clearly Shapiro wants to make sculpture that has the kind of inevitability that so much great sculpture has had and yet still insists upon the human dynamism and velocity of change that are facts of a technological age. Clearly, too, he wants the experience of dynamism and change to be grounded in the physical and psychological life of the body. His determination to keep rooting this experience in the concreteness of the body, and in the texture of everyday life, is part of what gives his sculpture its moral urgency and weight.

III

While it is impossible in one essay to adequately explore the meanings of Shapiro's work, it is important to consider some of the other implications of the ways in which it is put together and unfolds. Particularly those that suggest a kind of progressive thinking that does not sacrifice individualism, that does not let anyone off the hook, and that does not bow to any party line.

Shapiro's sculpture is fundamentally populist. Its imagery is familiar. The gestures and feelings it embodies are no one's property. There is no emotion or action in it to which the vast majority of people cannot relate. Its movements cross borders, pointing toward a physical and spiritual soil that different races, classes, genders and nationalities share.

The states of feeling and being that are honored by Shapiro's sculptures do not exist in a hierarchical relationship to one another. Sadness, joy, depression, exhilaration, all coexist in a way that makes it clear that they are all inescapable and valid. The human capacity for delight, ecstasy and nobility is unequivocally acknowledged by Shapiro's figures; but so is the capacity for conflict, violence and domination. In Shapiro's world, each individual has the potential to be or do anything. No human response or movement can be seen in isolation; each gains meaning in relation to another. Grace and despair, anxiety and delight, cruelty and tenderness are all part of the life of the body. To deny any one of them is to be blind to history and to the fullness and complexity of the self. It is also to limit the possibilities of the creative imagination.

Because Shapiro's figures are forever in flux, moving from action to action, emotion to emotion, they resist traditional notions of monumentality, which tend to rely, like Rodin's great sculpture *Balzac*, on a seamless presence. In Shapiro's work, sculptural conviction derives from the eccentric yet irrefutable joining of multiple selves. The Shapiro figure is often disjunctive. Sometimes it is hard to imagine how the body coheres with its limbs pulling it this way and that. Shapiro does extol the individual, but it is an individual that is unsettled and in perpetual transition. It is not a force of domination. It is a force of empathy. The fact of fluidity and the gift of concentration may or may not produce a sense of monumentality. They are capable of producing a sense of grandeur that Rodin and Giacometti surely would have recognized even though they knew it was not their own.

It is just as essential to recognize that in Shapiro's figures the body can always be reimagined. Shapiro is a highly kinesthetic sculptor. He does not just show bodily states. He wants viewers to experience them: he wants the marching and tumbling and fighting and praying to be known by the viewer's body. He is exceptionally good at projecting a thrust or dropping a volume so that the body of the viewer feels itself being thrown outward or collapsing. He has the keenest sculptural sense since Matisse of the body's center of gravity in the hip and pelvic area, and he can play off it in ways that argue that a conventional experience of the body is not inevitable. He may be the only contemporary sculptor who can join a vertical or diagonal rectangle to the legs in such a way that the unexpected movement of the hip in relation to the legs is experienced as both dislocated and natural.

Shapiro encourages viewers to experience parts of their bodies both in terms of where they are known to be and in terms of where they might be in another time and space. He creates a kinesthetic identification with legs and shoulders as they are joined in fact; but by enabling viewers to experience offbeat and unpredictable joinings of limbs to trunk, and trunk to head, he also uses kinesthetic identification to challenge the normal experience of the body. He makes unexpected relationships within the body seem essential to an understanding of sculptural and human freedom.

This is individualism of a thoughtful and challenging kind. It depends upon attentiveness to the physical and psychological mechanisms of the individual body and a commitment to the body as a site and source of freedom. It encourages empathy, concentration and openness to the child in the adult and the adult in the child and to all sides of the human whole. During a period in which the individual tends to be either dumbly mythified or all but drowned in a sea of context and determinism, it throws its weight toward the complexity and mobility of the self and the lyricism and drama of the embodied soul. And even if Shapiro does not want his sculpture to be put in the service of ideas of social progress and transformation, the presence of a wide-open and unimaginable future is alive and well in it. The ability to make people think about the individual in thoughtful and challenging ways was one of the achievements of Rodin, Matisse and Giacometti. It may be that it is only by working within the tradition of figurative sculpture that such a challenge can be formulated in contemporary art with comparable intelligence and flair.

ENDNOTE

1. All quotations are taken from Peter Boswell's interview with Joel Shapiro in "Joel Shapiro: Outdoors," catalogue for exhibition at the Walker Art Center in Minneapolis, June 4, 1995, to March 15, 1996, and at the Nelson-Atkins Museum of Art in Kansas City, April 20 to October 13, 1996, pp. 27-40.

Michael Brenson is an independent critic, curator and scholar living in New York. He has written extensively on twentieth-century sculpture.

untitled, 1995, cast bronze, 1/3, 111¾ x 69 x 45″

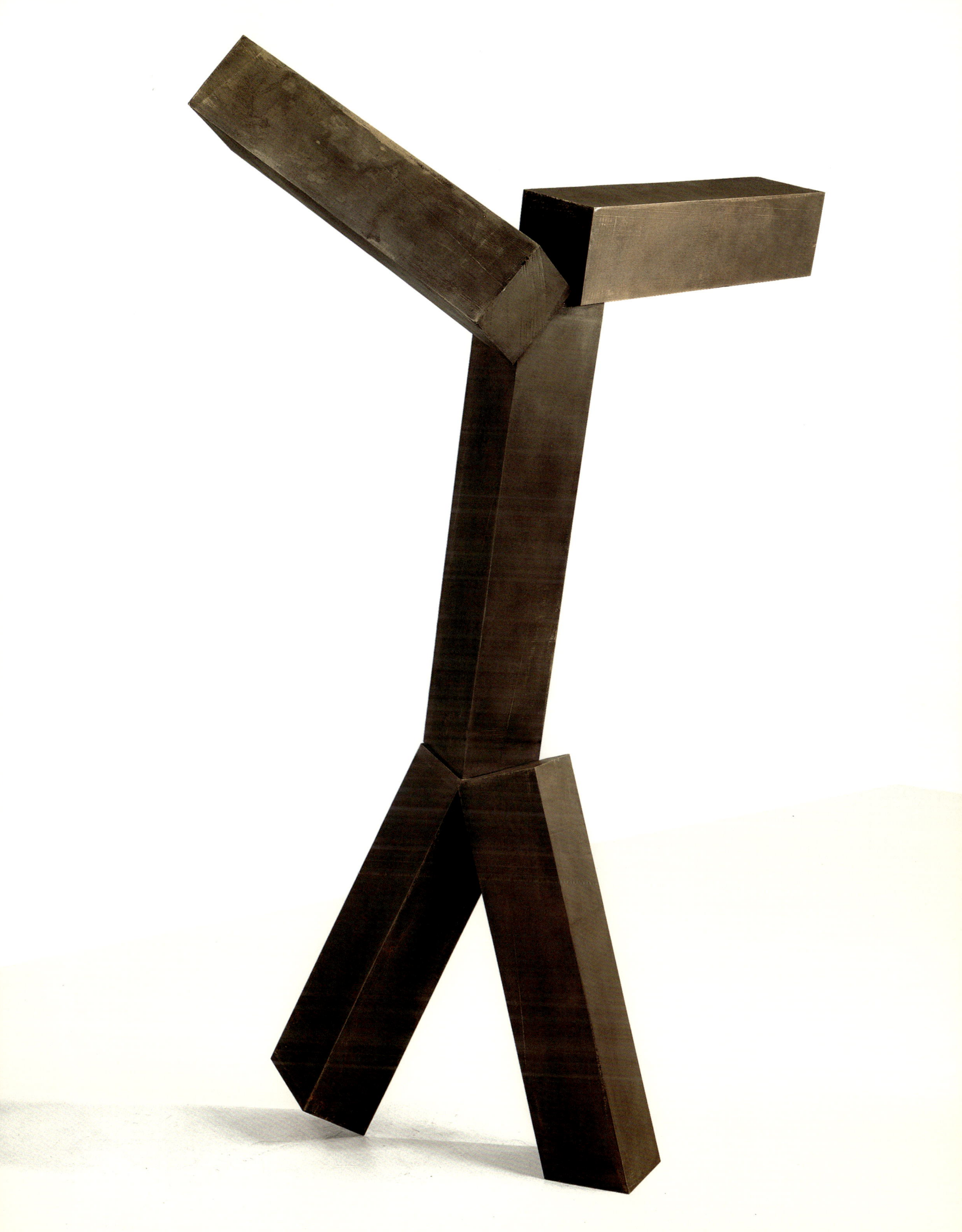

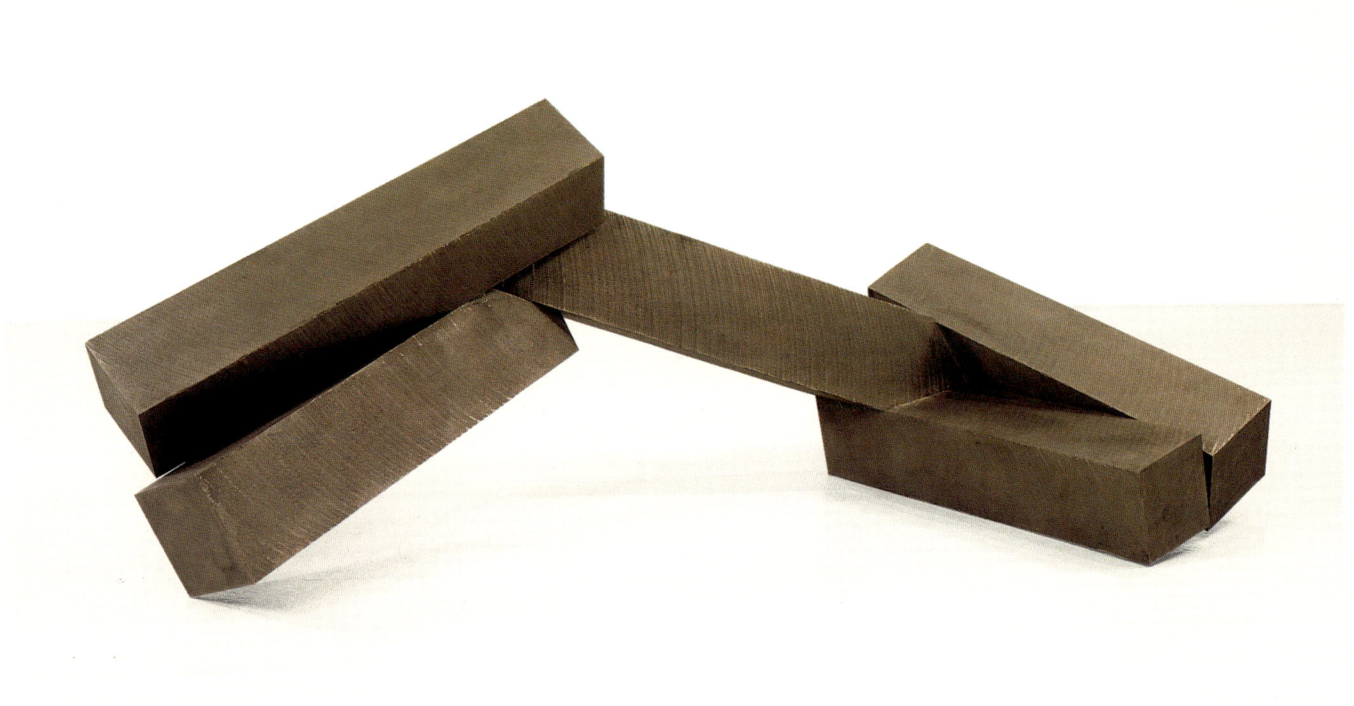

    untitled, 1994-95, cast bronze, 1/3, 36 x 48 x 83″

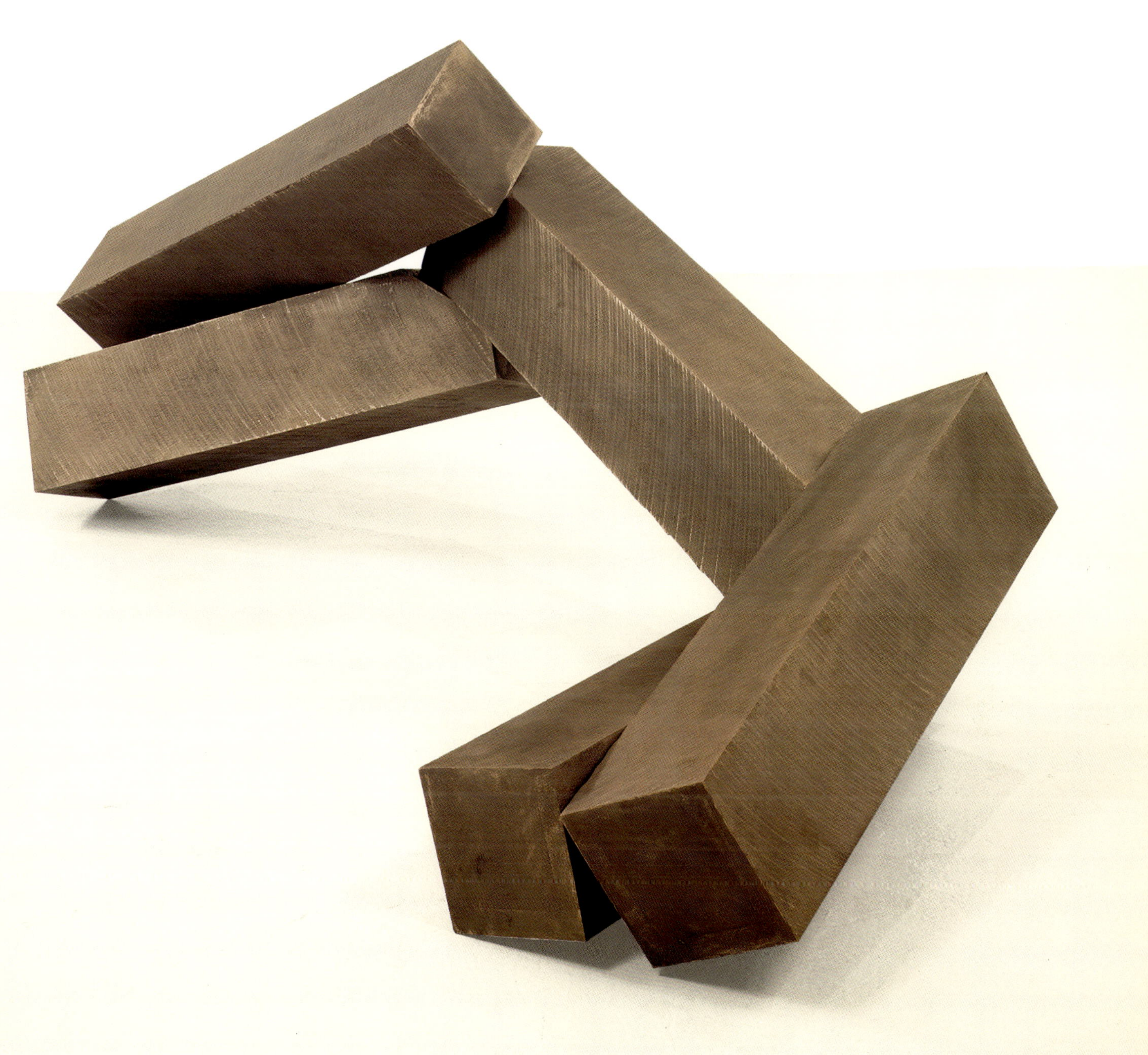

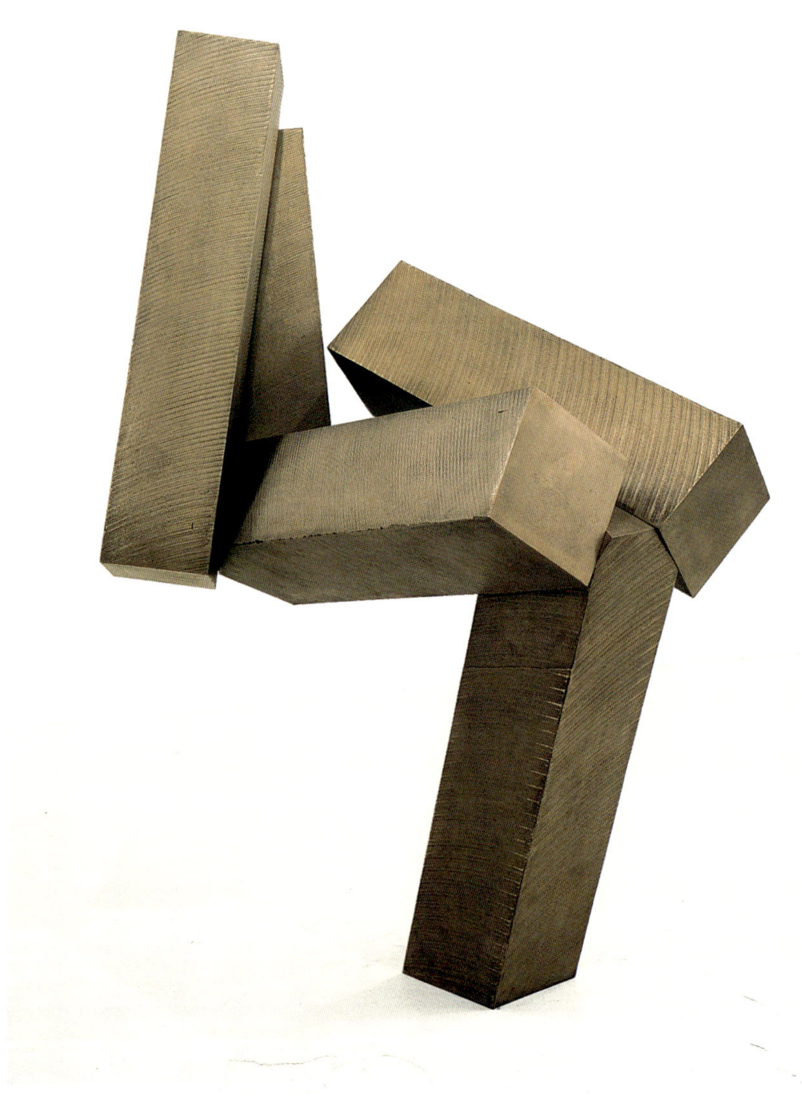

    untitled, 1994-95, cast bronze, 1/3, 68¼ x 54 x 28½″

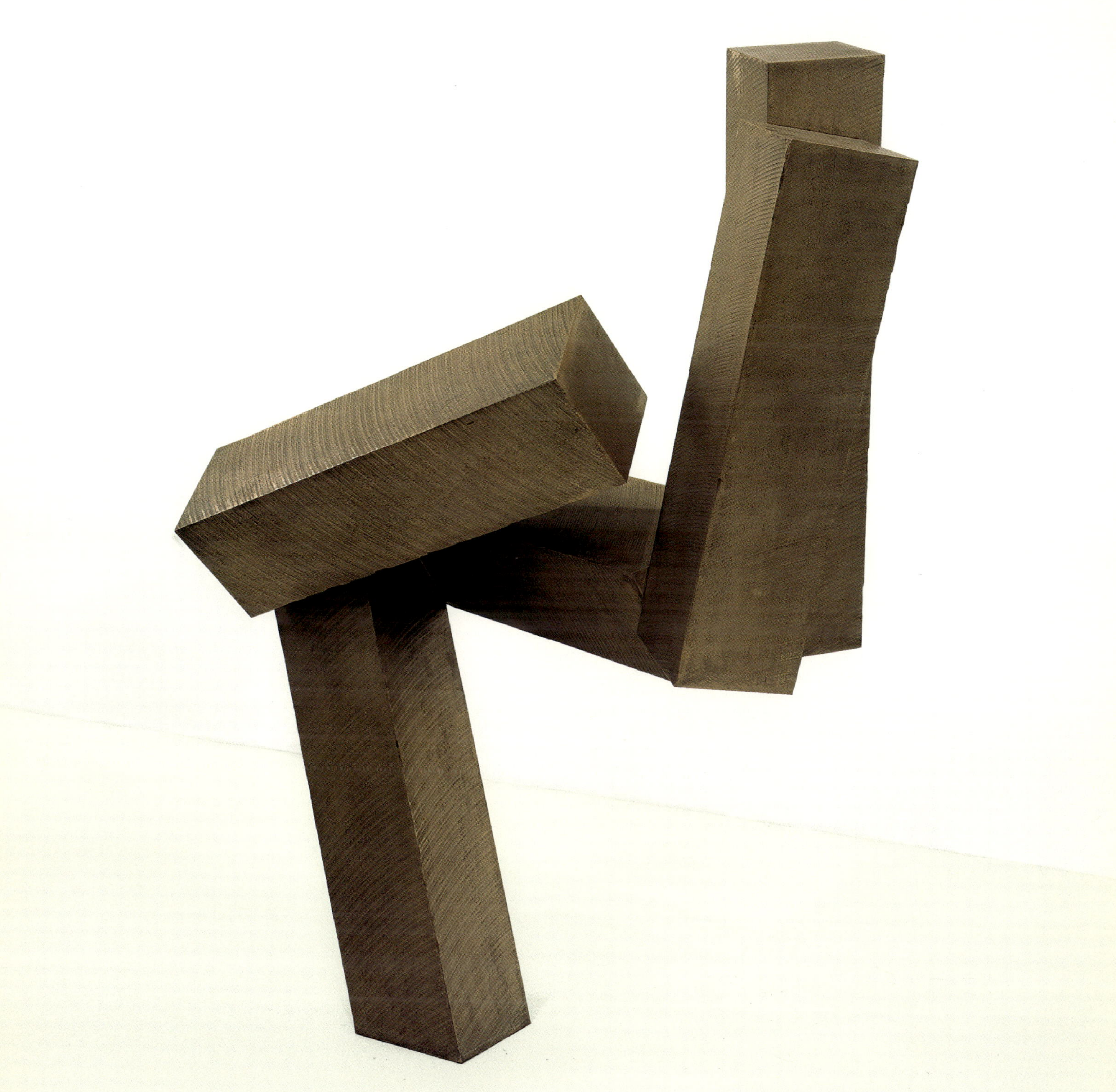

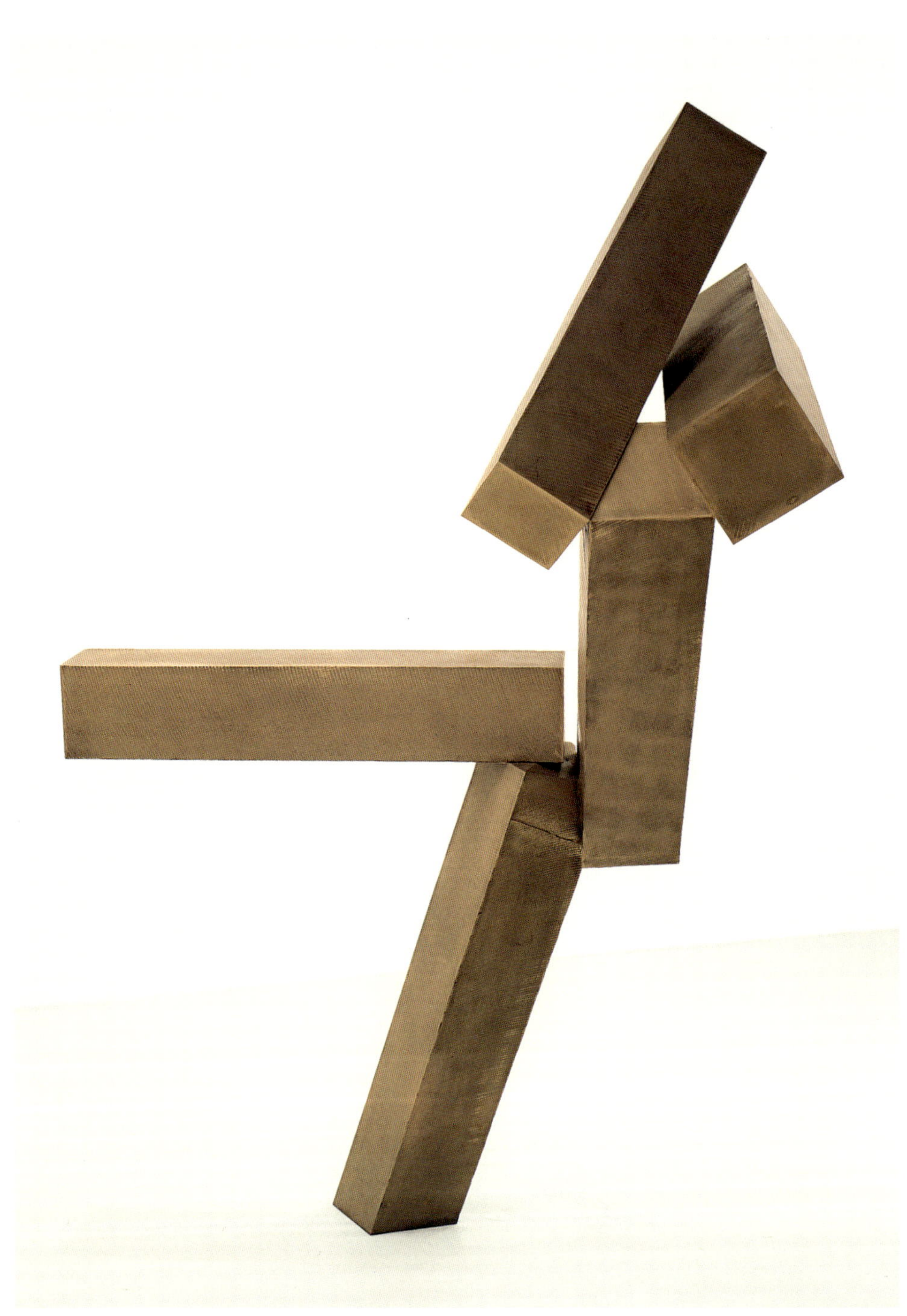

untitled, 1994-95, cast bronze, 2/4, 98 x 68 x 65″

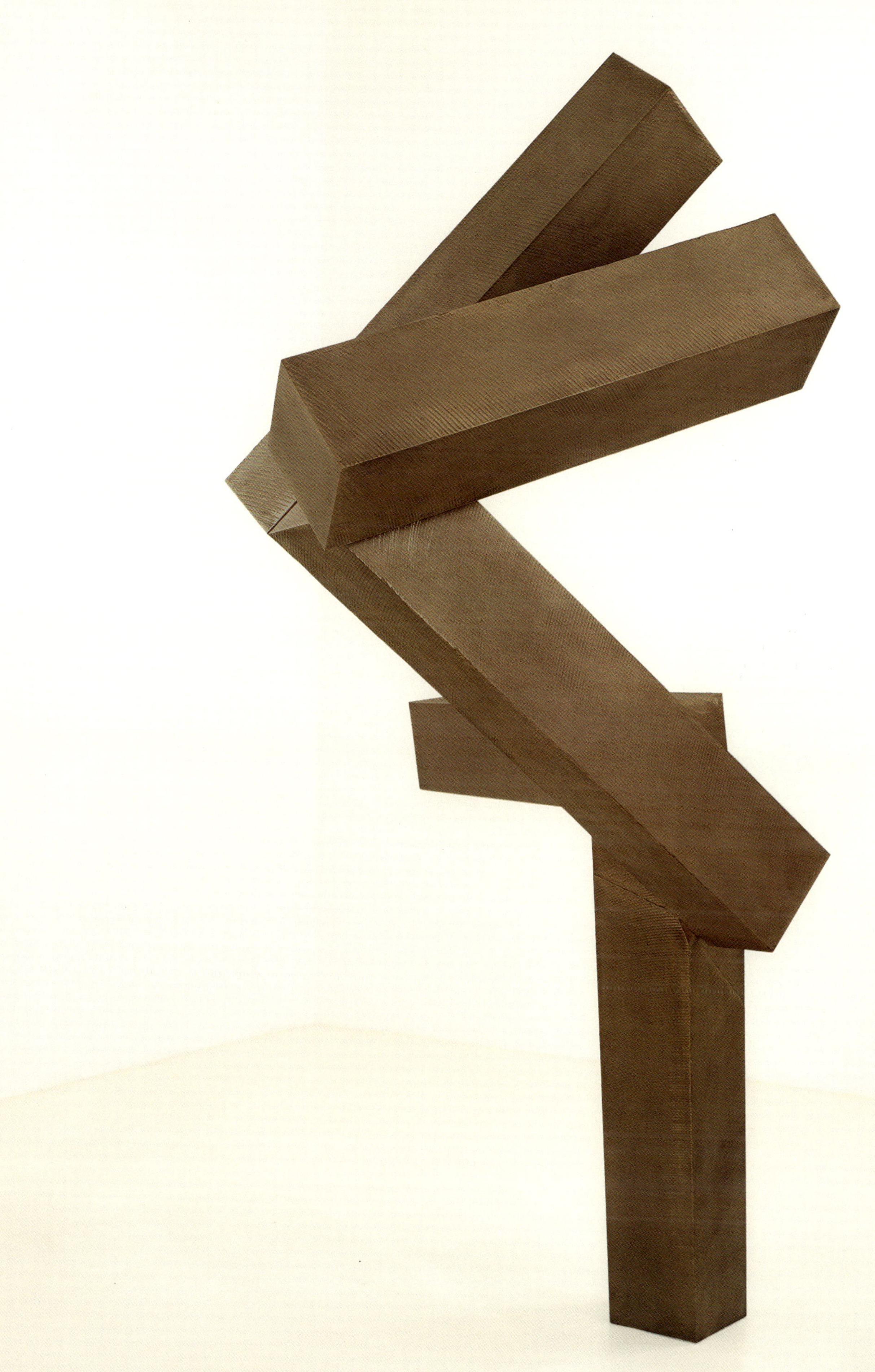

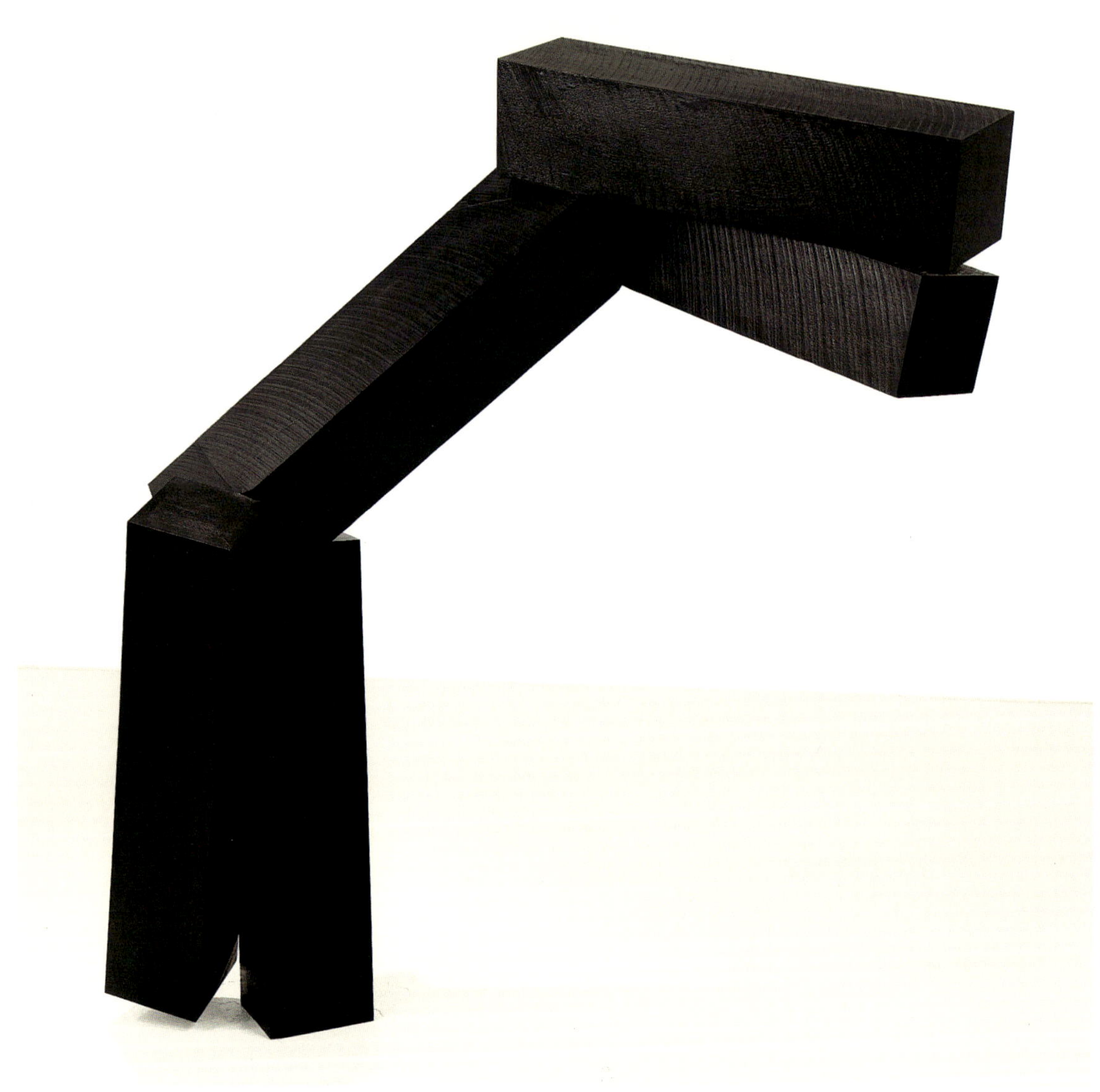

untitled, 1995, cast bronze, 1/3, 75 x 71 x 41″

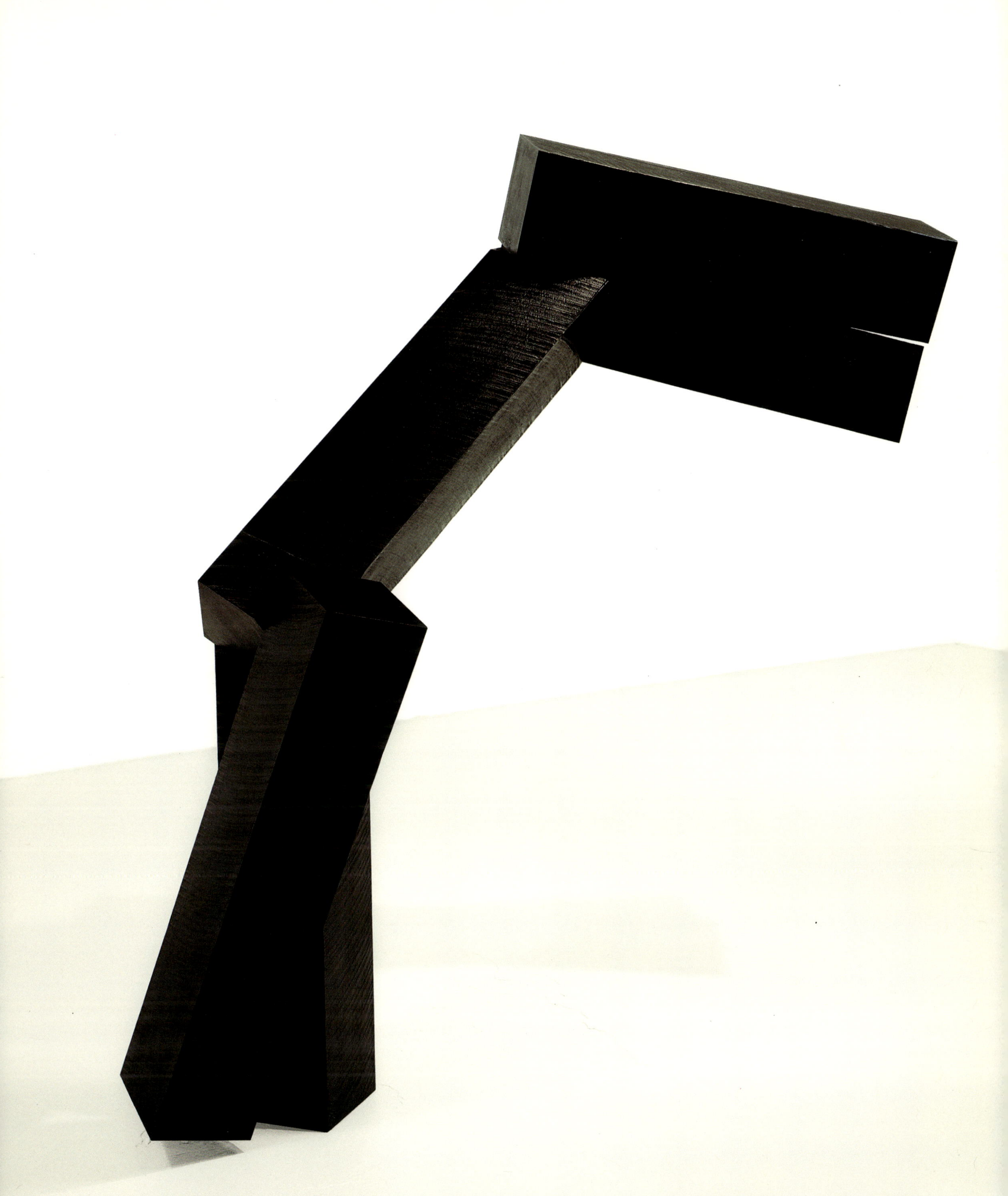

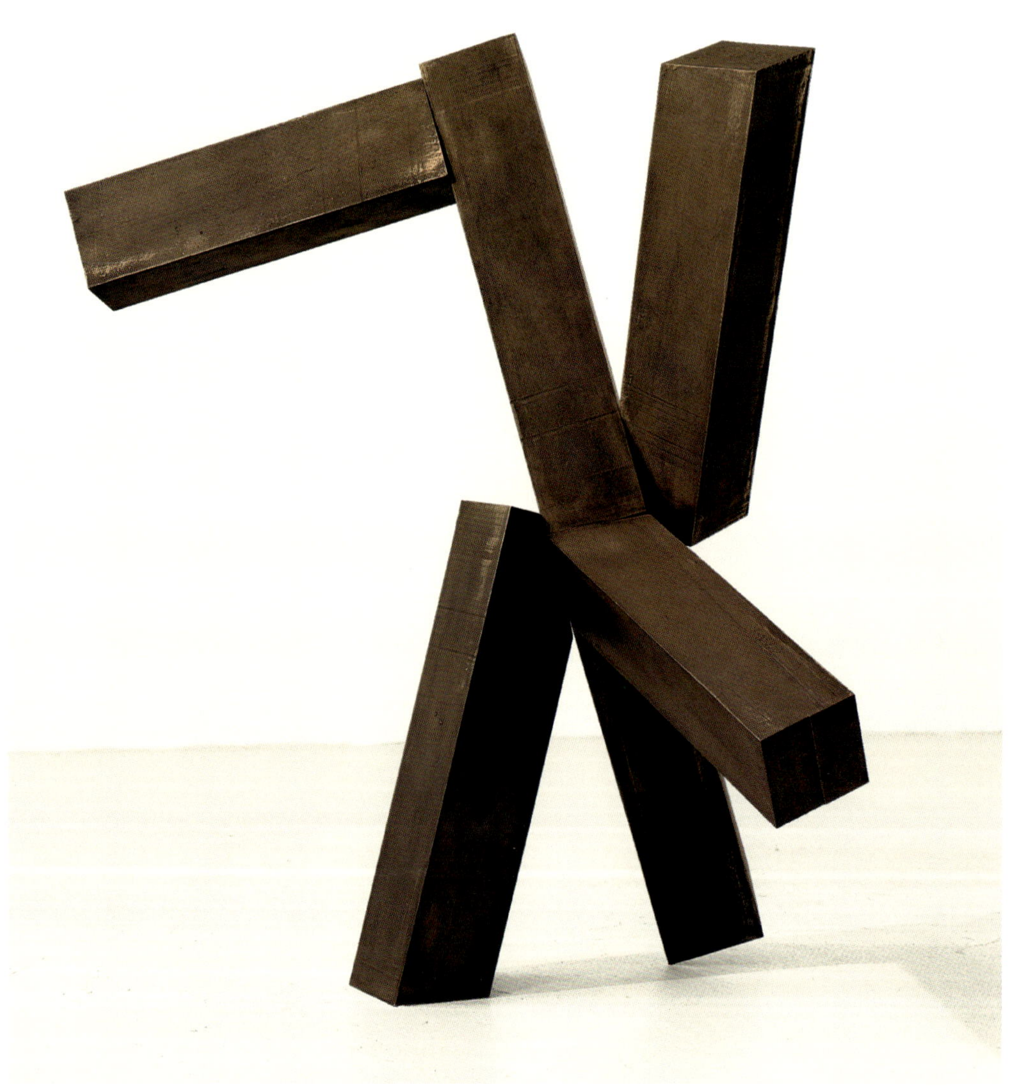

untitled, 1995, cast bronze, 1/4, 71 x 70 x 45″

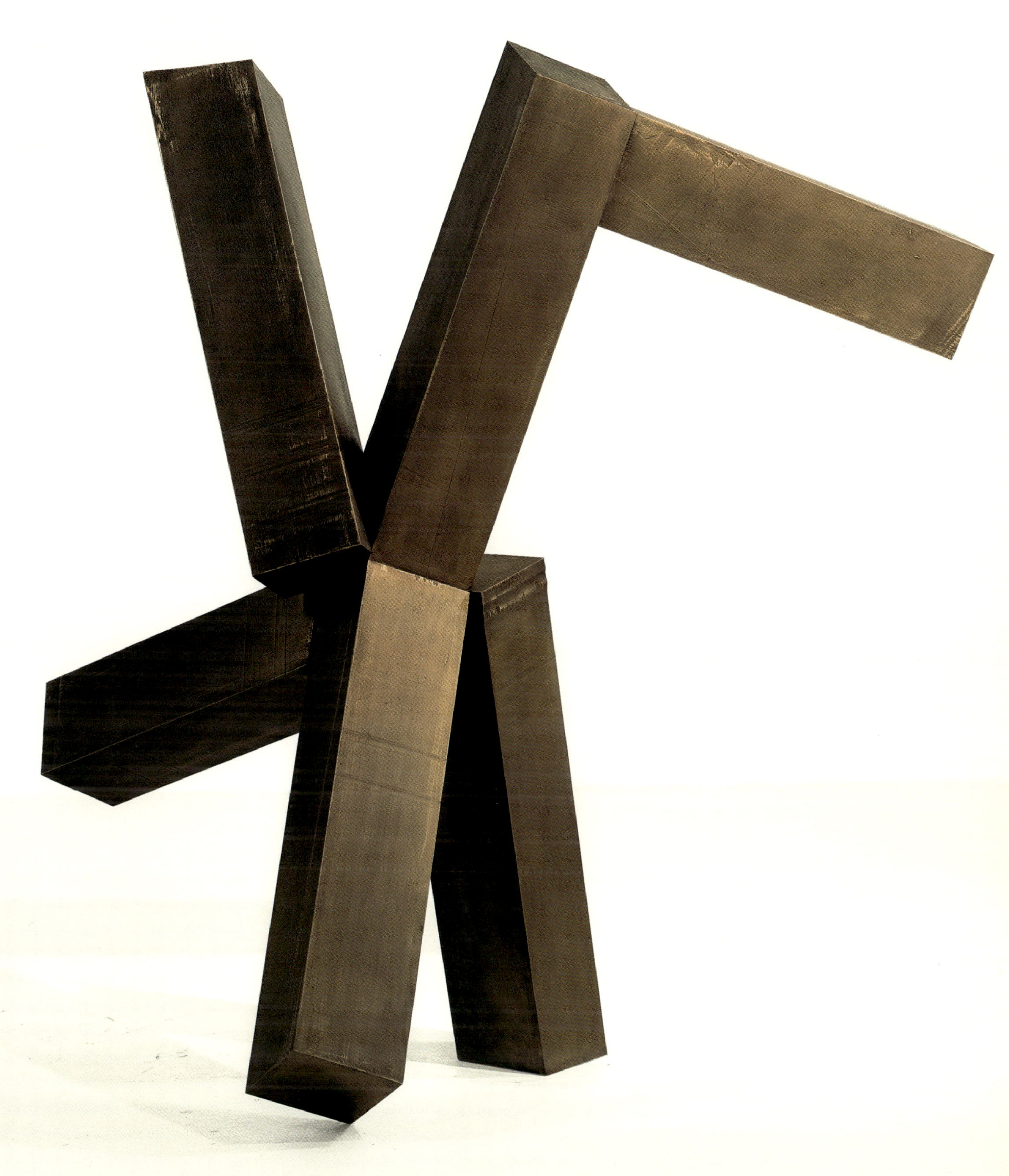

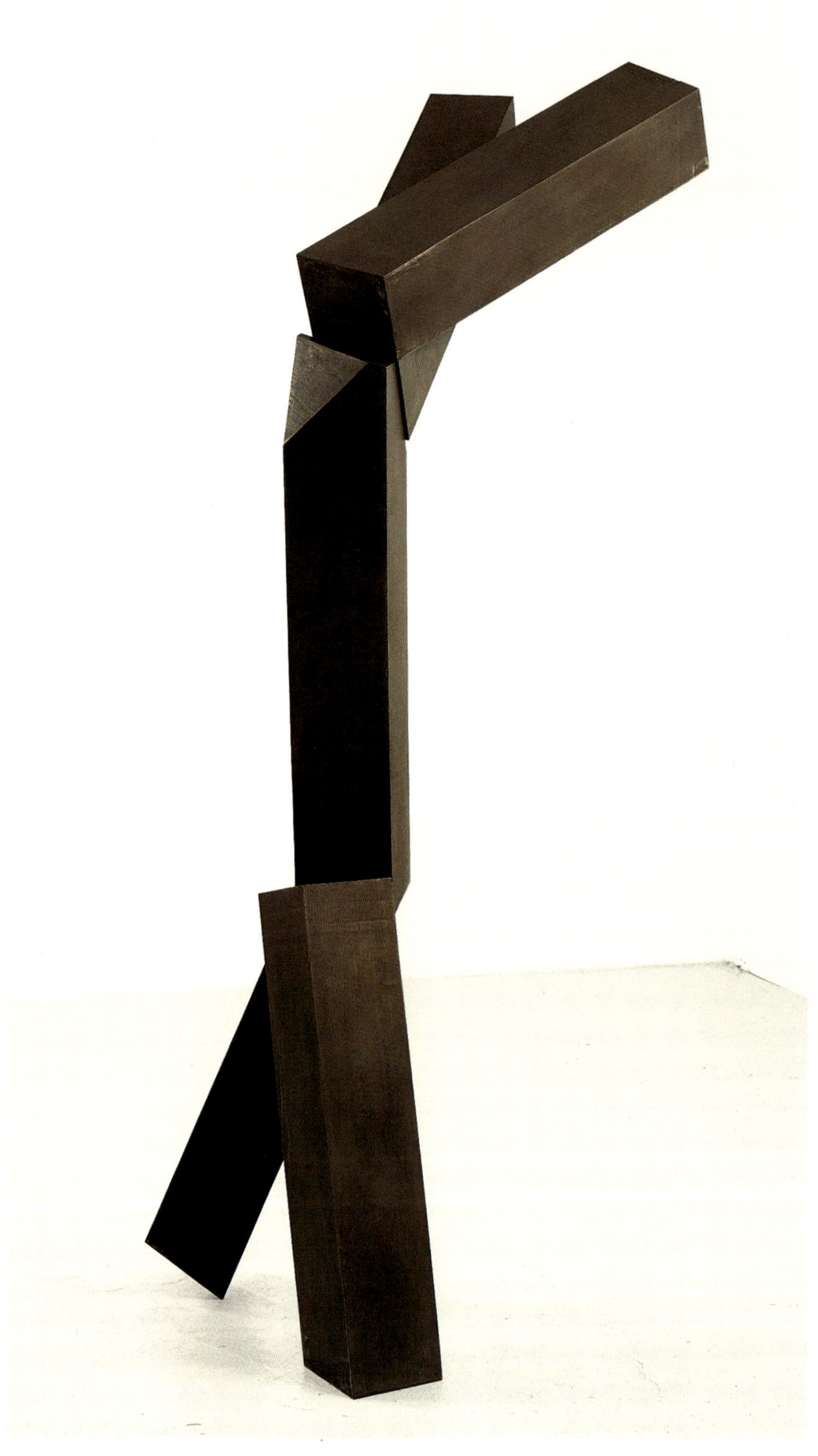

untitled, 1995, cast bronze, 1/3, 111 x 50 x 38″

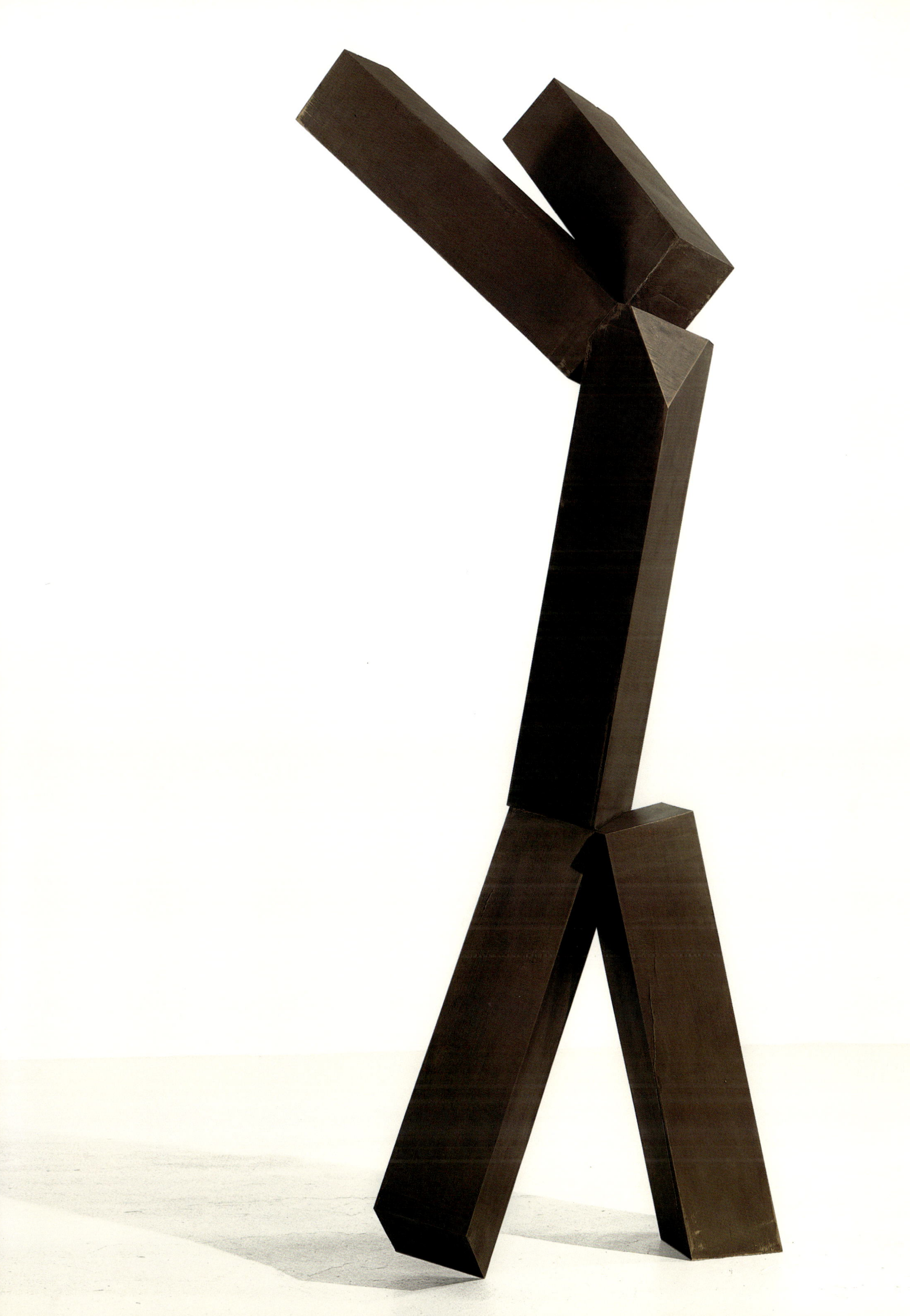

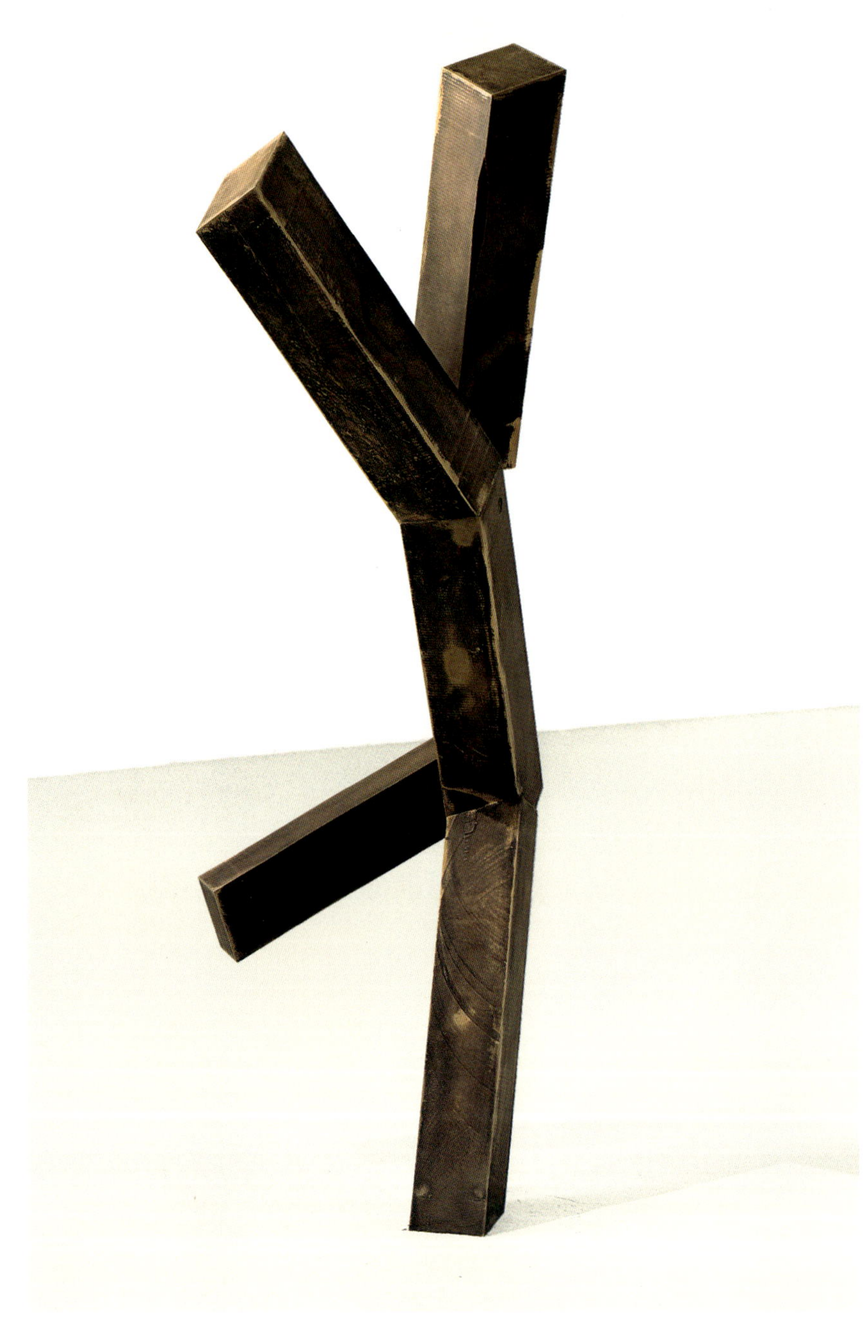

untitled, 1995, cast bronze, 1/4, 66½ x 37 x 26″

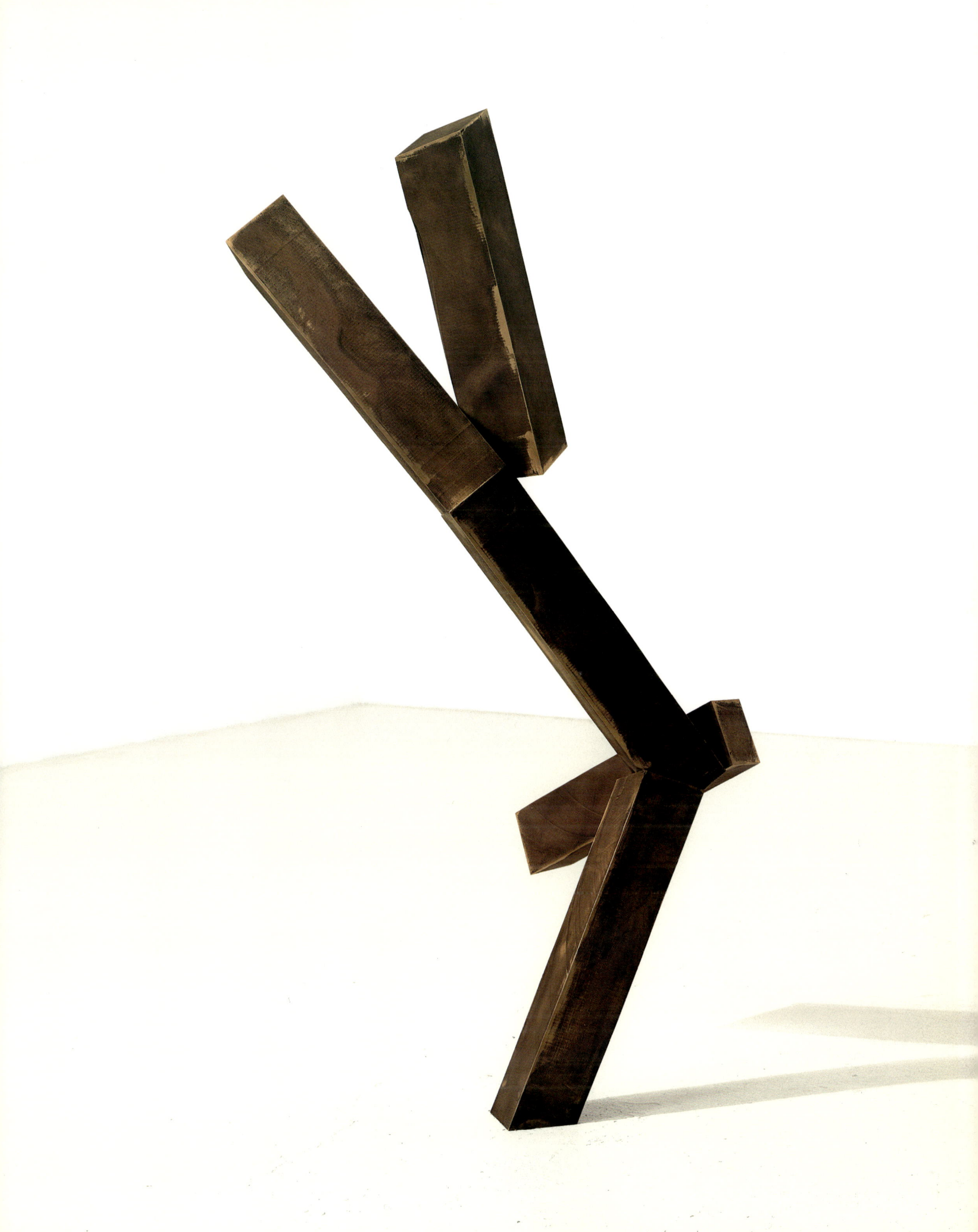

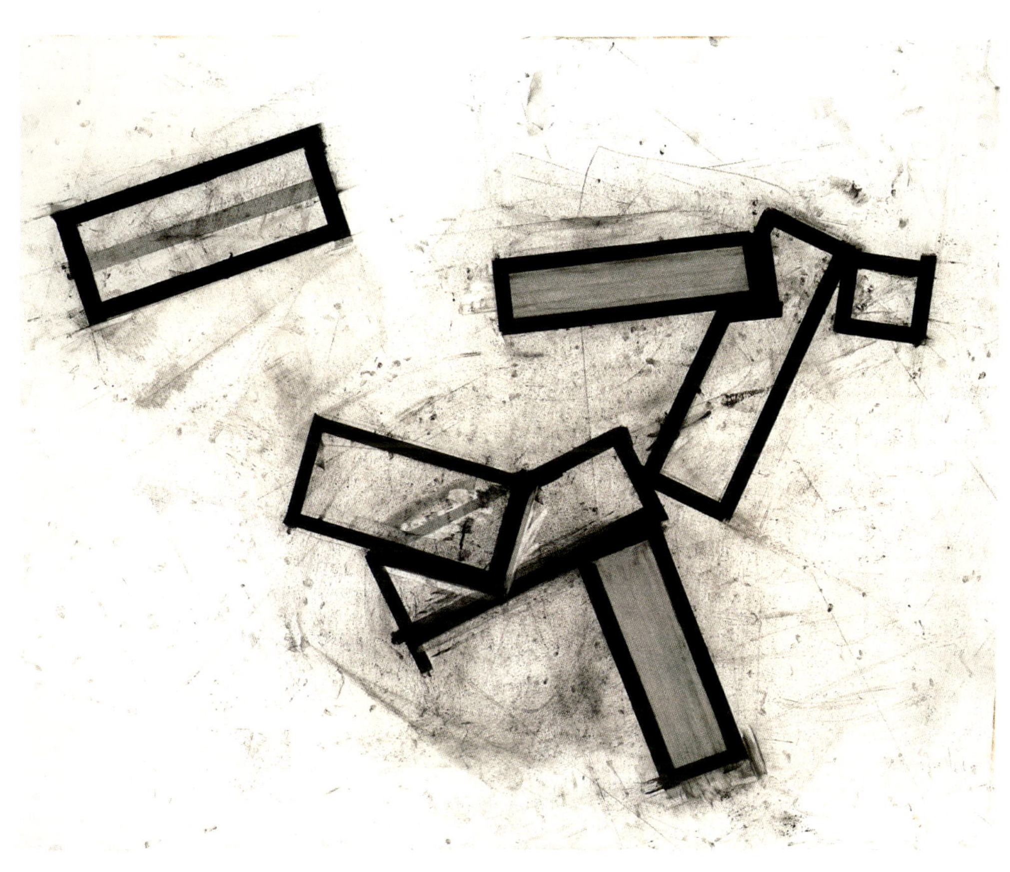

untitled, 1996, charcoal on paper, 40 x 49″

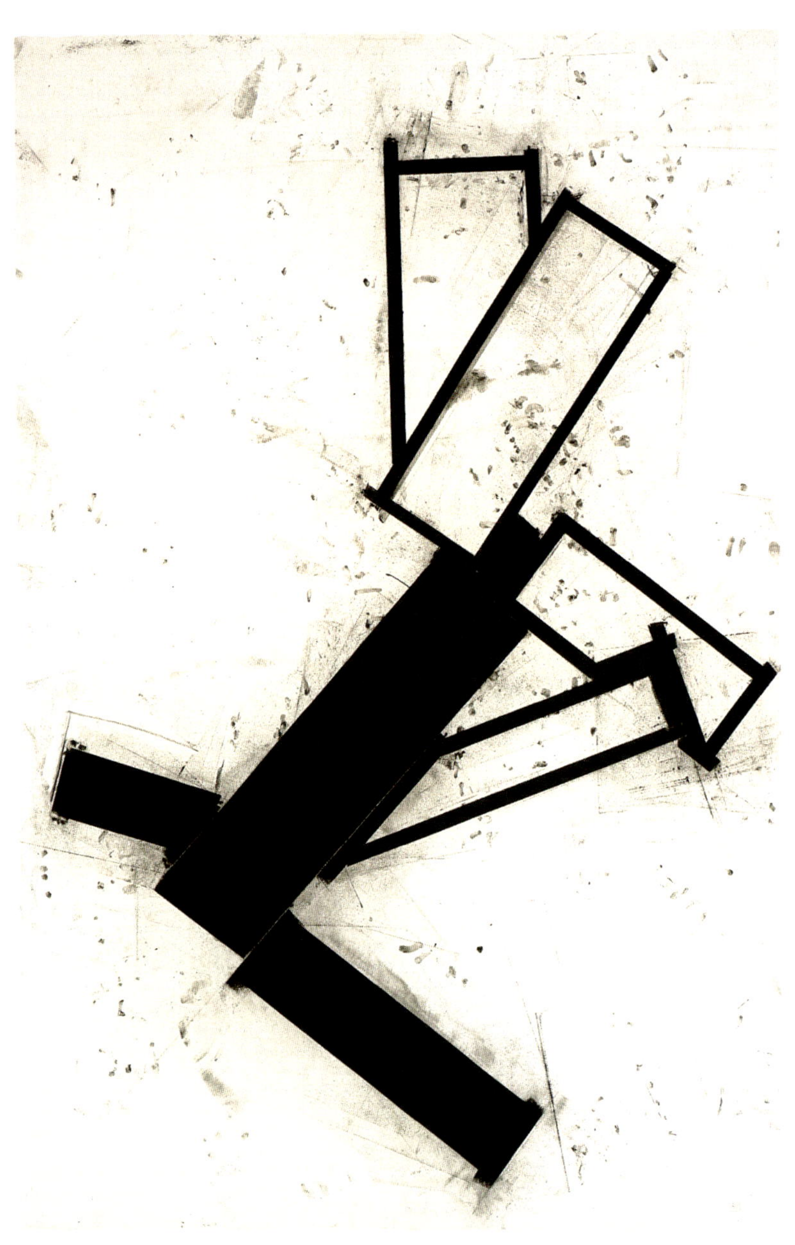

   untitled, 1996, chalk and charcoal on paper, 60¼ x 40"

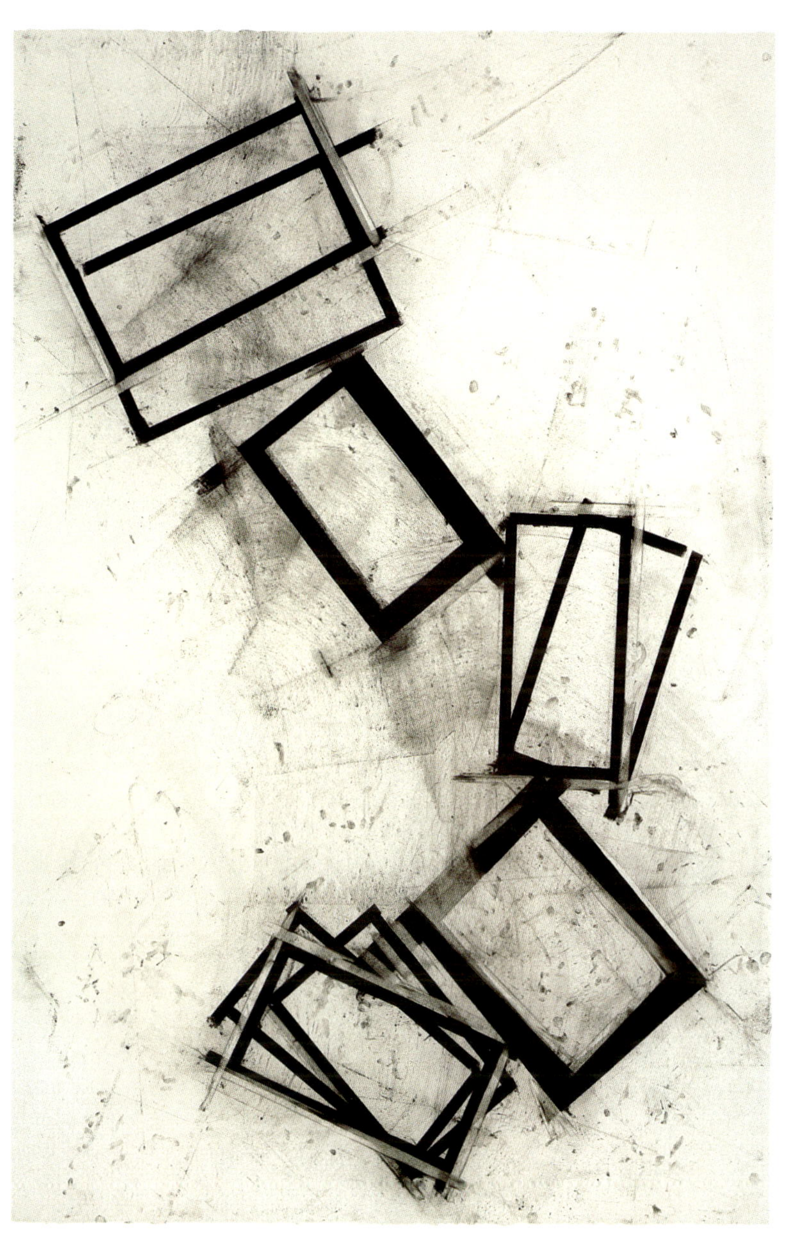

untitled, 1996, chalk and charcoal on paper, 60¼ x 40″

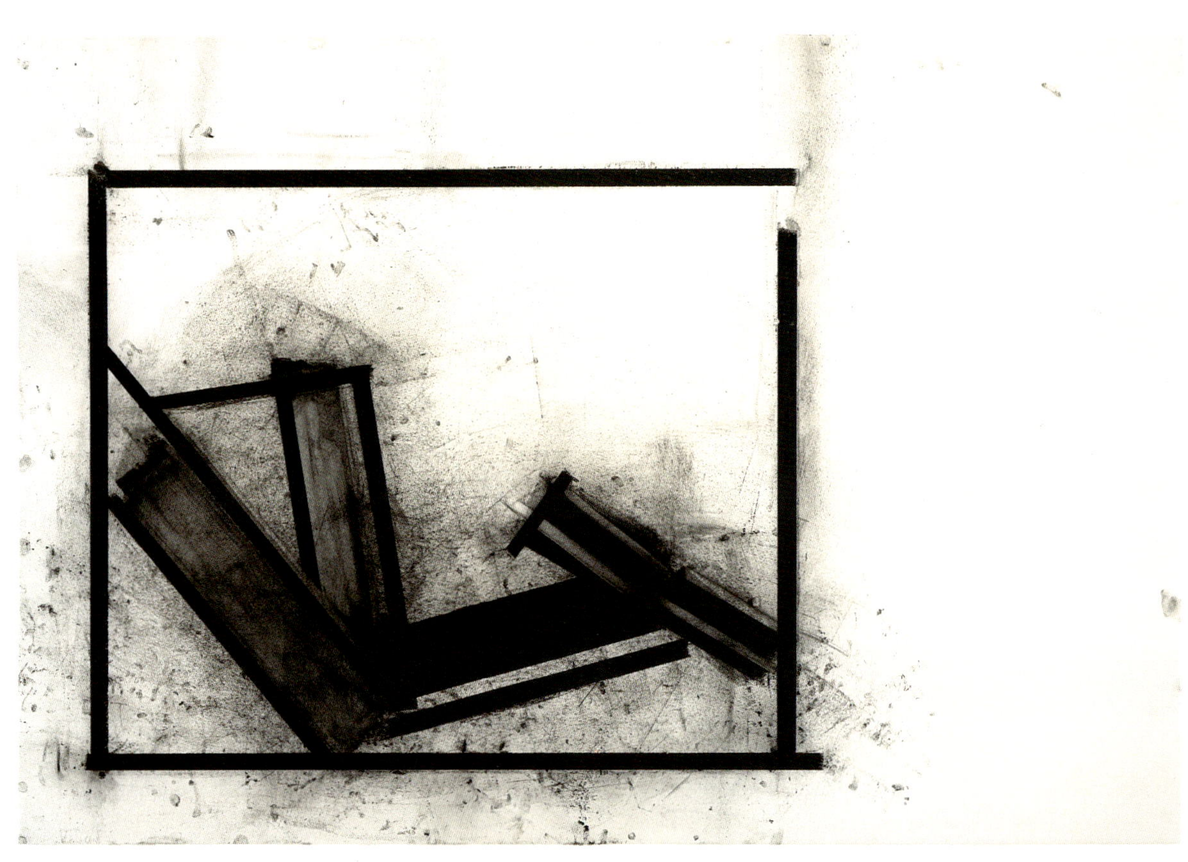

 untitled, 1996, charcoal on paper, 40¼ x 59¾″

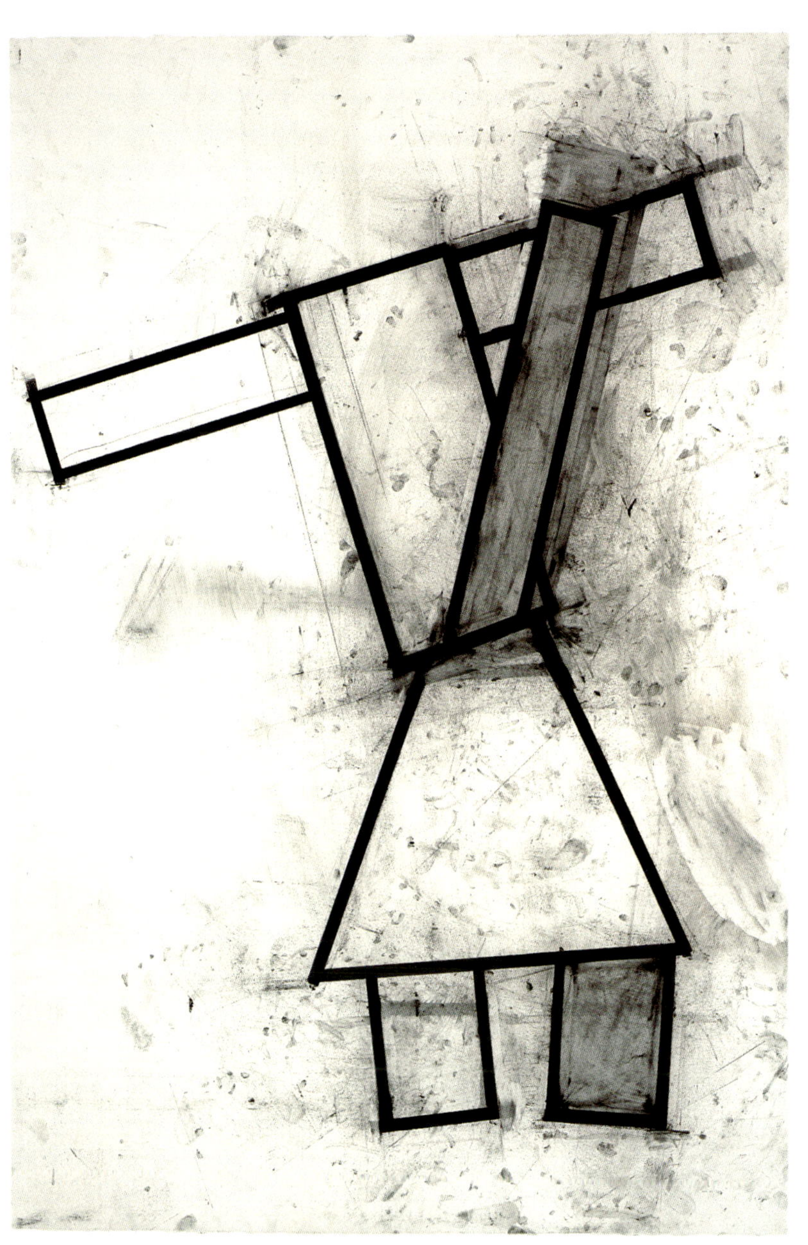

untitled, 1996, chalk and charcoal on paper, 60¼ x 40"

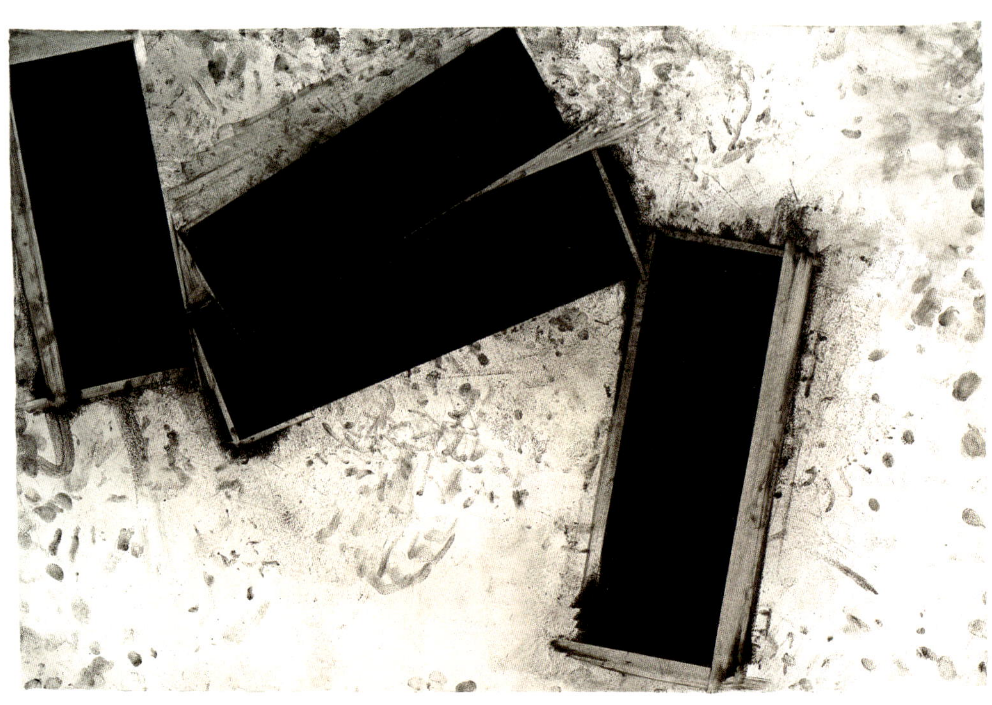

untitled, 1996, chalk and charcoal on paper, 26 ⅞ x 40 ⅛″

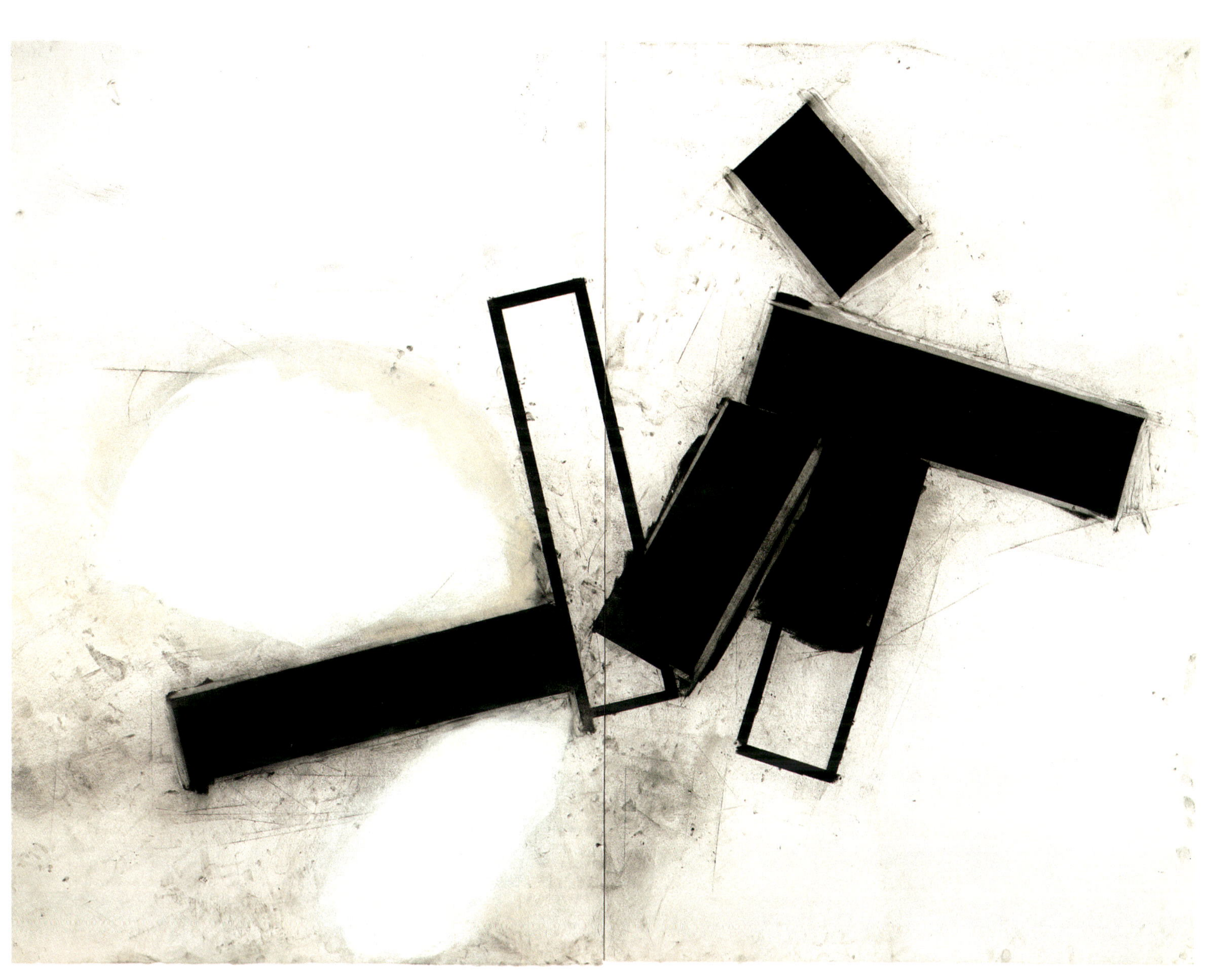

untitled, 1996, chalk, charcoal and pastel on paper, two sheets, 60¼ x 40″ each; 60¼ x 80″ overall

LIST OF REPRODUCTIONS

untitled, 1995, cast bronze, 1/4, 71 x 70 x 45″
cover

untitled, 1995, cast bronze, 1/3, 111¾ x 69 x 45″
page 15

untitled, 1994-95, cast bronze, 1/3, 36 x 48 x 83″
pages 16-17

untitled, 1994-95, cast bronze, 1/3, 68¼ x 54 x 28½″
pages 18-19

untitled, 1994-95, cast bronze, 2/4, 98 x 68 x 65″
pages 20-21

untitled, 1995, cast bronze, 1/3, 75 x 71 x 41″
pages 22-23

untitled, 1995, cast bronze, 1/4, 71 x 70 x 45″
pages 24-25

untitled, 1995, cast bronze, 1/3, 111 x 50 x 38″
pages 26-27

untitled, 1995, cast bronze, 1/4, 66½ x 37 x 26″
pages 28-29

untitled, 1996, charcoal on paper, 40 x 49″
page 31

untitled, 1996, chalk and charcoal on paper, 60¼ x 40″
page 32

untitled, 1996, chalk and charcoal on paper, 60¼ x 40″
page 33

untitled, 1996, charcoal on paper, 40¼ x 59¾″
page 34

untitled, 1996, chalk and charcoal on paper, 60¼ x 40″
page 35

untitled, 1996, chalk and charcoal on paper, 26⅞ x 40⅛″
page 36

untitled, 1996, chalk, charcoal and pastel on paper, two sheets,
60¼ x 40″ each; 60¼ x 80″ overall
page 37

BIOGRAPHY

BORN

1941   New York, New York

AWARDS

1975   Visual Arts Fellowship, Visual Arts Program, National Endowment
       for the Arts

1984   Brandeis University Creative Arts Award

1986   Skowhegan Medal for Sculpture

1990   Award of Merit Medal for Sculpture, American Academy and
       Institute of Arts and Letters, New York

ONE-PERSON MUSEUM EXHIBITIONS

1973   The Clocktower, Institute for Art and Urban Resources, New York.

1976   Museum of Contemporary Art, Chicago.

1977   Albright-Knox Art Gallery, Buffalo, New York.

1979   Akron Art Institute, Akron, Ohio.

1980   *Joel Shapiro: Sculpture and Drawing*, Whitechapel Art Gallery,
       London. Traveled to Museum Haus Lange, Krefeld, Germany;
       and Moderna Museet, Stockholm.

1980   Bell Gallery, Brown University, Providence. Traveled to Georgia State
       University, Atlanta; and The Contemporary Arts Center, Cincinnati.

1981   The Ackland Art Museum, University of North Carolina, Chapel Hill.

1981   The Israel Museum, Jerusalem.

1982   Portland Center of the Visual Arts, Portland, Oregon.

1982   Whitney Museum of American Art, New York. Traveled to Dallas
       Museum of Fine Arts, Dallas; Art Gallery of Ontario, Toronto;
       and La Jolla Museum of Contemporary Art, La Jolla, California.

1985   Stedelijk Museum, Amsterdam. Traveled to Kunstmuseum Düsseldorf,
       Germany; and Staatliche Kunsthalle, Baden-Baden, Germany.

1986   Seattle Art Museum, Seattle, Washington.

1986   *Joel Shapiro: Sculpture and Drawings 1981-85*, The John and Mable
        Ringling Museum of Art, Sarasota, Florida.

1987   *Joel Shapiro: Painted Wood*, Hirshhorn Museum and Sculpture
        Garden, Washington, D.C.

1988   *Joel Shapiro: Recent Sculptures and Drawings*, Cleveland Museum
        of Art, Cleveland.

1989   *Playing with Human Geometry: Joel Shapiro's Sculpture*, The Toledo
        Museum of Art, Toledo, Ohio.

1990   *Joel Shapiro Skulptur & Grafik 1985-1990*, Museet i Varberg,
        Varberg, Sweden.

1990   *Joel Shapiro: Tracing the Figure*, Des Moines Art Center, Des Moines.
        Traveled to Baltimore Museum of Art, Baltimore; and Center for the
        Fine Arts, Miami.

1990   Louisiana Museum for Moderne Kunst, Humlebaek, Denmark.
        Traveled to IVAM Centre Julio González, Valencia, Spain; Kunsthalle
        Zürich, Switzerland; and Musée des Beaux-Arts, Calais, France.

1991   *Joel Shapiro: Selected Drawings 1968-1990*, Center for the
        Fine Arts, Miami.

1995-96 *Joel Shapiro: Outdoors*, Walker Arts Center/Minneapolis Sculpture
        Garden, Minneapolis. Travels to The Nelson-Atkins Museum of
        Art/Kansas City Sculpture Park, Kansas City.

PUBLIC COLLECTIONS

The Ackland Art Museum, University of North Carolina, Chapel Hill, North Carolina

Albright-Knox Art Gallery, Buffalo, New York

Art Gallery of Ontario, Toronto, Canada

Art Museum of South Texas, Corpus Christi, Texas

Australian National Gallery, Canberra, Australia

The Baltimore Museum of Art, Baltimore, Maryland

British Museum, London, England

The Brooklyn Museum, Brooklyn, New York

Centre Georges Pompidou, Paris, France

Cincinnati Art Museum, Cincinnati, Ohio

The Cleveland Museum of Art, Cleveland, Ohio

Colby College Museum of Art, Waterville, Maine

The Corcoran Gallery of Art, Washington, D.C.

Dallas Museum of Art, Dallas, Texas

The Denver Art Museum, Denver, Colorado

Des Moines Art Center, Des Moines, Iowa

The Detroit Institute of Arts, Detroit, Michigan

The Douglas S. Cramer Foundation, Los Angeles, California

Eli Broad Foundation, Los Angeles, California

Fogg Art Museum, Harvard University, Cambridge, Massachusetts

Grand Rapids Art Museum, Grand Rapids, Michigan

Hakone Open-Air Museum, Hakone-machi, Japan

Hall Family Foundation on permanent loan to The Nelson-Atkins Museum of Art, Kansas City, Missouri

High Museum of Art, Atlanta, Georgia

Hirshhorn Museum and Sculpture Garden, Smithsonian Institution, Washington, D.C.

Hood Museum of Art, Dartmouth College, Hanover, New Hampshire

Israel Musem, Jerusalem, Israel

IVAM Centre Julio González, Valencia, Spain

The John and Mable Ringling Museum of Art, Sarasota, Florida

Kunsthaus Zürich, Zürich, Switzerland

Lannan Foundation, Los Angeles, California

Los Angeles County Museum of Art, Los Angeles, California

Louisiana Museum for Moderne Kunst, Humlebaek, Denmark

The Menil Collection, Houston, Texas

The Metropolitan Museum of Art, New York, New York

Milwaukee Art Museum, Milwaukee, Wisconsin

Modern Art Museum of Fort Worth, Fort Worth, Texas

Moderna Museet Stockholm, Stockholm, Sweden

The Museum of Contemporary Art, Los Angeles, California

Museum of Contemporary Art, San Diego, California

Museum of Fine Arts, Boston, Massachusetts

The Museum of Fine Arts, Houston, Texas

Museum of Modern Art, Friuli, Italy

The Museum of Modern Art, New York, New York

The Nasher Collection, Dallas, Texas

National Gallery of Art, Washington, D.C.

The Newark Museum, Newark, New Jersey

North Carolina Museum of Art, Raleigh, North Carolina

The Parrish Art Museum, Southampton, New York

Philadelphia Museum of Art, Philadelphia, Pennsylvania

The Picker Art Gallery, Charles A. Dana Arts Center, Colgate University, Hamilton, New York

Rose Art Museum, Brandeis University, Waltham, Massachusetts

The Saint Louis Art Museum, St. Louis, Missouri

Stedelijk Museum, Amsterdam, The Netherlands

Tate Gallery, London, England

Tel Aviv Museum of Art, Tel Aviv, Israel

The Toledo Museum of Art, Toledo, Ohio

University of Nebraska, Sheldon Memorial Art Gallery and Sculpture Garden, Lincoln, Nebraska

University Gallery, University of Massachusetts, Amherst, Massachusetts

Walker Art Center, Minneapolis, Minnesota

Weatherspoon Art Gallery, University of North Carolina, Greensboro, North Carolina

Wexner Center for the Arts, Ohio State University, Columbus, Ohio

Whitney Museum of American Art, New York, New York

RECENT COMMISSIONS

1993   United States Holocaust Memorial Museum
Washington, D.C.
Architect: James Ingo Freed; Pei, Cobb, Freed & Partners

1994-95   Sony Plaza
New York, New York
Architect: Philip Johnson, Gwathmey Siegel and Associates Architects

1994-95   Friedrichstadt Passagen
Berlin, Germany
Architect: O.M. Ungers

1996   Kansas City International Airport
Kansas City, Missouri

SELECTED EXHIBITION CATALOGUES

Chicago, Museum of Contemporary Art. *Joel Shapiro.* 1976.
Essay by Rosalind Krauss.

London, Whitechapel Art Gallery. *Joel Shapiro: Sculpture and Drawing*. 1980.
Essay by Roberta Smith.

Providence, Brown University, Bell Gallery. *Joel Shapiro*. 1980.
Essay by William Jordy.

Jerusalem, The Israel Museum. *Joel Shapiro*. 1981.
Essay by Stephanie Rachum.

New York, Whitney Museum of American Art. *Joel Shapiro*. 1982.
Introduction by Richard Marshall, essay by Roberta Smith.

Amsterdam, Stedelijk Museum. *Joel Shapiro*. 1985.
Essays by Marja Bloem and Karel Schampers.

Sarasota, The John and Mable Ringling Museum of Art.
Joel Shapiro: Sculpture and Drawings 1981-85. 1986.
Essay by Mark Ormond.

Washington, D.C., Hirshhorn Museum and Sculpture Garden.
Joel Shapiro: Painted Wood. 1987.
Essay by Ned Rifkin.

Tokyo, Gallery Mukai. *Joel Shapiro*. 1988.
Essay by Lynne Cooke.

London, Waddington Galleries. *Joel Shapiro*. 1989.
Introduction by Lynne Cooke.

Valencia, IVAM Centre Julio González. *Joel Shapiro*. 1990.
Essays by Nancy Princenthal and Rosalind Krauss.

Des Moines, Des Moines Art Center. *Joel Shapiro: Tracing the Figure*. 1990.
Essay by Donald Kuspit, interview by Deborah Leveton.

Miami, Center for the Fine Arts. *Joel Shapiro: Selected Drawings 1968-1990*. 1991.
Essay by Mark Ormond, interview by Paul Cummings.

New York, The Pace Gallery. *Joel Shapiro: Sculpture and Drawings*. 1993.
Essay by Peter Schjeldahl.

New York, PaceWildenstein, *Joel Shapiro: Painted Wood
Sculpture and Drawings*. 1995.
Interview by Ellen Phelan.

Minneapolis, Walker Art Center, and Kansas City, Nelson-Atkins Museum of Art.
Joel Shapiro: Outdoors. 1995.
Essay by Deborah Emont Scott, interview by Peter Boswell.

Photography:
Sarah Harper Gifford, p. 34
Ellen Page Wilson, cover, pp. 15-33, 35-37

Catalogue design and production:
Tomoko Makiura and Paul Pollard

ISBN: 1-878283-60-X